GUIDES TO EVERYTHING

Research your Family Tree and discover your ancestors

By Natasha Reed

ISBN: 978-1-84678-009-7

Copyright 2006, Quick123 Limited

Quick123 Limited, PO Box 45092, London N4 2ZJ.

Website: www.quick123.co.uk

Customer service or additional copies can be sought at service@quick123.co.uk.

Letter to the Reader

Have you ever wondered who your great-great-grandparents were? Perhaps you are related to royalty or someone famous!

Tracing your family history (known as genealogy) is an increasingly common and enjoyable way to uncover the past.

Now, with the help of the Internet and computer wizardry, you can trace your family, search through archives, retouch old photos, track down the meaning of your surname - and much more.

While this process in itself can be very interesting, you can also use the information you uncover in a fun way. You might draw a family tree or create a scrapbook.

Don't worry if you think you are not very good at writing or you don't know where to start. All it takes is a bit of effort and enthusiasm... and this guide.

So, congratulations. By reading this book you are taking the first step on your amazing journey to uncovering the secrets of your past.

Natasha Reed

Contents

Quick123 Limited
PO Box 45092
London N4 2ZJ

Email: peterpurton@quick123.co.uk

Dear Quick123 reader

Thank you for buying this guide. We hope you enjoy reading it.

Our aim is to help you achieve the goals you set yourself, whether it's getting a better job, improving relationships or creating a better you. And to help you achieve that without costing you too much time, effort or money.

Because you, the reader, are at the centre of everything we do, we'd like to hear from you. Whether you have comments about this book, ideas for a new topic or issues in your life you feel we might be able to help with, send us an email or a letter.

If we take up any of your ideas to create a new title we'll make sure you get your own special copy.

We want to provide you with the kinds of guides you want to read. With your help, I'm sure we can.

Happy reading,

Peter Purton
Quick123 Limited

Start gathering evidence

If you are aiming to trace your past, start with what you know: the full names and dates of birth of all your immediate family. Then work backwards.

A simple way to record your results is by using a drop-line chart, or pedigree (as shown). For more information on drawing your family tree, see the guide near the back of the book.

You now need to decide which ancestral line to focus on; for example your mother's line (maternal or distaff) or your father's (paternal).

You could do both, but at the beginning it is easier to choose one to research.

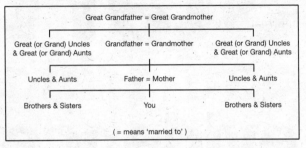

Stick to one line, which could be a male line with the same surname. Wives who marry into the family will form part of the story too.

You might not want to feature your own surname or maiden name but might start with your great-grandmother's maiden name. Alternatively, you might look at your partner's ancestry.

You also need to decide if you will write the story in chronological order - will you go forwards or backwards? You could start from a point in the past or work back from the present day. As you go along, arrange your material in order according to which chronological sequence you use.

So, to start your family tree, you need a single chronological listing of events that are relevant to your family. But how do you go about finding this information?

• Write down anything that you can remember personally. Record all important dates such as birth and baptism, education, work, marriage, etc. Record your own biography if it is going to form part of the story

• Draw up a list; talk to relatives and close family friends to obtain first-hand accounts, memories and stories, especially from older generations. Don't wait until it's too late: when they're gone their memories will have too

Take notes and compile a list of questions you want answered. Jot down any family legends or traditions, which can then be examined for any grain of truth. Don't dismiss anything until you have researched it, but don't take anything at face value either.

TOP TIPS

Interviewing Tips

- Respect peoples' homes if visiting them

- Respect peoples' wishes not to re-visit the past if requested

- Always be polite and kind

- Make it clear that you are not after the inheritance, but merely information

- Stop the interview if the interviewee shows signs of tiredness or distress - you can always come back another time after they've had a rest

- Be sensitive and never judge past situations by today's standards - circumstances would have been different then

- Record the interview if possible, for later reference

- Take round a portfolio of family photos if possible

- Don't call on the elderly (particularly ladies) at any time, but especially at night, without having arranged it beforehand

- Look through old correspondence, photos, letters, diaries, heirlooms and other material that can find its way into trunks, drawers, attics or cellars. You will be amazed at the amount of information you can extract from these objects.

  Don't discard anything; even a pair of cufflinks can be useful if engraved. Mark the back of photographs clearly with names and dates so that you don't forget anything

- Try to establish where your family is from; this will play an important role in where to look for relevant records. You might have copies of birth, marriage or death certificates which will help you trace your history back further. If not, find out how you can order copies by visiting www.familyrecords.gov.uk

- See if anyone else has done any research. People can often provide you with details of names, dates and key family events - but never take anything at face value. It will be your job to investigate family myths

  Remember to record each piece of information as you discover it. It doesn't matter whether you use a computer or index cards and folders, as long as the information is legible and kept in order.

  Decide which method you will use at the start and stick to it. If you don't find anything, record it as a 'negative search' so you don't cover the same ground again.

QUESTIONS TO ASK YOUR FAMILY

It is much better to interview elderly relatives than to write to them, as they might not be able to see or write very well. Give some thought to the questions you want to ask your family before you start.

What sort of information are you aiming to find out? Jot down names and dates as a reminder. You might want to take along photographs or a family tree of what you know so far. Try these sample questions as a starting point but add any other relevant ones you have.

- Is there a family Bible, giving dates of special events?

- Are there any certificates of birth, marriage or death that you know of?

- Did the family come from a certain town or county, or did they emigrate?

- Where did members of the family go to school?

- Did anyone serve in the forces - army, navy, air force, marines?

- Can you remember the trade/occupation of *(insert name)*?

"Give some thought to the questions you want to ask before you start"

- I remember *(insert name)*; what are your memories of them?

- Do you recognise any of the people in this photograph? (show photograph)

- Do you have any photographs of older members of the family? If not, could you describe the physical appearance of *(insert name)*?

- Does the family have a motto that you know of?

- Has anyone researched the family history before?

SAMPLE QUESTIONNAIRE

If you can't visit someone to interview them, it might be worthwhile sending them a questionnaire to fill in if they have time.

Here is a sample questionnaire to send them. Amend as required, then photocopy/write out as many times as needed for each person.

Your father's name:..
His date of birth:...
Where born:...
His school(s): (dates)..
His career (jobs in order):..
....
Was he in the army/navy/air force?....................................
Regiment, ship, squadron:...
Where did he serve?...
Where did he live (please give dates):................................
....
Date of death:..
Where:..
Where buried:..
Date of marriage:...
Where:..

(similar details for your mother)
(list of and dates for any children)

How to Start Searching

Once you have collected as much background information as possible, you are ready to start searching for concrete evidence. Most of your research will take place in archives, local studies libraries or specialist family history centres (see the specialist centres section).

So what sort of thing are you searching for? Basically you are looking for information about the people you are investigating.

Start with basic information such as their date and place of birth, marriage and death, any different addresses, what their occupation was, etc. For this, you will need to find primary sources - original records made by someone who knew the truth of what was happening at the time in question.

You could use civil registration records of births, marriages and deaths; census returns; parish registers; non-parochial records and tax records. Electoral registers will be of use to trace movement from one address to another. However, remember that women were only eligible to vote from 1919.

Surnames

You will need to pay particular attention to surnames. Beware: most of them will have varied significantly over the centuries. They could be affected by local dialect, intonation, spelling errors and a variety of other factors.

You might like to contact an organisation called the Guild of One-Name Studies (GOONS for short) to discover if anyone else is collecting references to surnames which interest you. Write to: The Registrar, GOONS, Box G, 14

Charterhouse Buildings, Goswell Road, London EC1M 7BA.

Alternatively, search the Genealogical Research Directory (GRD). As the world's largest listing of surname queries, this is a key reference work for family historians. Edited by Keith Johnson and Malcolm Sainty, it has been published annually since 1982. It is now also available on CD-ROM.

Once you have found a name in the list which interests you, use the number beside it to establish the name and address of the relevant subscriber from a separate list.

When you write to the subscriber, mention the edition in which you found your reference and give the subscriber's number. Make sure your letter is concise and include a stamped addressed envelope.

Another source that may help is the British Isles Genealogical Register (known as the BIG R). This was published in 1994 by the Federation of Family

History Societies and was researched by over 17,000 family historians worldwide.

The register for England is published in county sections. It is available on microfiche from various record offices and libraries.

Photographs

Whilst looking for information, you should also hunt for photographs: it is much more interesting to put names to faces. Search local newspapers for photographs; these should be available from the turn of the century onwards.

Record offices, museums, local studies libraries and reference libraries will usually have collections of old photos. Local history societies may also be worth approaching. If you're unsure of the date a photo was taken, search the image for hidden clues such as the style and fashion of clothing, surroundings, etc.

Golden rules for research

- Never assume - check family stories against proven facts

- Keep all notes in a notebook to keep it safe; never rely on memory

- Systematically record all research undertaken - keep it separate so you can find things instantly. For example, census entries, registers and wills can all be kept in separate files

- Double-check all your findings

- Take note of everyone, even servants, as they may turn out to be family. Witnesses at weddings will often be family members

- If writing to people for help or advertising, never reveal your mother's full maiden name if that is what you use for bank identification purposes

- Be careful about posting family information publicly. Never reveal too much about your personal address, such as your home address, or when you are out

Wise Words

It's no use seizing on a famous person or titled family with a name like yours and trying to prove a link between you. Always work back from yourself

For example, people called Shakespeare cannot be descended from William. He had one son who died and his married daughters' descendants petered out

Specialist Centres

Now that you know what you are looking for, where do you need to go? Here are some of the best places to start.

If you are not used to places such as these, they can initially appear daunting. Usually there will be someone there to help you get started, however.

- The Family Records Centre (FRC) in London provides access to some of the most important sources for family history research in England and Wales, including birth, marriage and death certificates from 1837 and census returns from 1841 to 1901

Births, marriages and deaths only started being recorded by the government in the late 1830s -

this is known as civil registration. To trace your family back into previous centuries you will need to look at Parish records

The FRC is the only place in England and Wales where the complete census returns for England and Wales can be found. FRC, 1 Myddelton Street, London EC1R 1UW, 0208 392 5300. Before you visit you need to be prepared. Visit **www.familyrecords.gov.uk/frc** before you go. The website also gives a variety of other links you may follow

• The General Register Office (GRO), part of the Family Records Office in London, is a central repository for all registered births, marriages and deaths in England and Wales. For those looking for records of adoption, there are counsellor services available if required

You may consult the indexes to birth, marriage and death records free of charge, but to obtain a certificate giving full details of any specific event you must fill in an application form and pay a fee

- The National Archives holds historic records (archives) created or collected by central government of the UK and central English law courts. The National Archives (Public Records Office), Ruskin Avenue, Kew, Richmond, Surrey, TW9 4DU, 0208 876 3444, www.nationalarchives.gov.uk

- The Borthwick Institute of Historical Research in York has a large collection of specialist records for family historians to view. Borthwick Institute, University of York, Heslington, York YO10 5DD, 01904 321166, www.york.ac.uk/inst/bihr

- New Register House in Edinburgh houses the civil registration records and Old Parish Registers (OPRs) for the whole of Scotland. You can also consult the 'statutory registers' of births, marriages and deaths whilst you are on the premises

  You will have to pay a fee to enter the centre. New Register House, Edinburgh EH1 3YT

- The General Register Office in Dublin holds records for Ireland to 1922, and southern Ireland only from 1922. General Register Office, Joyce House, 8-11 Lombard Street East, Dublin 2

- The General Register Office for Northern Ireland is at 49-55 Chichester Street, Belfast BT1 4HL. You can find birth and death registers for the counties of Northern Ireland from 1864, but marriages only from 1922

- Census returns can be viewed at The National Archives of Ireland (Bishop Street, Dublin 8) or The Public Record Office of Northern Ireland (66 Balmoral Avenue, Belfast BT9 6NY, Northern Ireland)

- The largest collection of newspapers in the United Kingdom is at The British Library Newspaper Library, Colindale Avenue, London NW9 5HE

Before you go

It is often a good idea to contact an archive before visiting: they usually require you to bring some form of identification and may be able to help you before you even get there.

Many county record offices have compiled basic name indexes, and it is a good idea to check these first in case you uncover immediate references to an ancestor.

Do your homework

Make sure you are prepared before visiting these centres. This will allow you to get the most out of them.

Talk to relatives to see what they have in their possession before you go. You don't want to pay for a birth certificate, only to discover your grandmother had one all along.

If you know your ancestors worked for a particular gentry family, you can find out if there are any estate papers for that family. Or if you know that any member of the family was an innkeeper or printer or butcher, a licence might have been issued.

Practical matters

Don't take too much luggage with you, even though some centres provide lockers. If possible, leave the children at home. Do not take pets, food or drink.

When visiting county record offices, you may be asked to take some form(s) of identification, so it's best to find out beforehand. This is because there have been cases of theft and damage due to carelessness before.

In many record offices they will not allow ink near the documents. You will need to take pencils.

You might find it useful to devise a system for searching through information before your visit. Draw a simple table with columns for information needed. Tick it off as you go, to make sure you don't do the same bits twice.

"You may be asked to take some form(s) of identification, so it's best to find out beforehand"

Make sure you don't rush and miss things, and always replace records where they came from. Remember to wind microfilm reels to the beginning for the next user.

Finally, don't expect instant success - but don't give up either.

Checklist

- Notebook

- No young children, large bags, pets, food or drink

- List of information to look for

- Have you contacted the centre for information / opening hours beforehand?

- Have you turned off mobile phones and pagers?

- If visiting county record offices, do you have ID, if required, and pencils, not pens?

- Afterwards - have you left everything as you found it, and replaced items?

Other methods of getting information

If you are unable to visit specialist centres in person, there are other ways to find the information you need.

You can make a postal application to the GRO. Write to the Postal Application Office, Office for National Statistics, General Register Office, Smedley Hydro, Southport, Merseyside PR8 2HH, giving as many details as possible. Any search made by staff in the indexes is restricted to a five-year period.

Alternatively, you could use the services of a professional researcher. A professional genealogist or record agent will find a certificate for you for a small charge. This will obviously save you time and travel costs.

You will find advertisements for services like this in Family Tree Magazine, Practical Family History, Family History Monthly, Ancestors and the Society of Genealogists' Genealogists' Magazine (see the Further Reading section for more information).

"You can make a postal application to the GRO. Alternatively, you could use the services of a professional researcher"

You could also contact a local superintendent registrar; they all retain original birth, death and some marriage certificates, with indexes.

Using
the
internet

The internet can be an invaluable tool when researching your family history. It can enable you to find information from places that you might be unable to visit in person or make contact with people in other countries, without leaving your own home.

Be careful not to rely totally on the internet, though. Always cross-check information with other sources.

Here are some helpful websites for beginners. But don't be afraid to do your own searching on the web.

- If your ancestors are from overseas, try www.movinghere.org - a database of digitised photographs, maps, documents and more, taken from archives that record migration experiences of the last 200 years

- For a beginner's guide to discovering your family history, visit www.familyrecords.gov.uk It contains invaluable information, ranging from the best sites to different sources

- A great genealogical site for the UK and Ireland is www.genuki.org.uk This is a 'virtual reference library', with information provided by knowledgeable volunteers

- The BBC has a good website with a handy guide to beginning your search. It includes case studies, expert advice and a regional map for uncovering local history. Visit the website www.bbc.co.uk/history/familyhistory/index.shtml

- One of the biggest free genealogy websites is www.rootsweb.com This site contains a whole host of information such as helpful search engines and information for getting started

- Find out information about your ancestors at the website of the Church of the Latter-Day Saints, www.familysearch.org

- In a similar vein to the ever-popular Friends Reunited website, there is now also www.genesreunited.co.uk

- www.familyrelatives.org allows you to download, print and view family history records

- www.cyndislist.com contains a massive number of genealogy links on the internet. Whatever you're looking for, you should find it here

- www.1837online.com offers facsimiles of all GRO birth, marriage and death indexes since 1837, searchable for a fee

- Order English and Welsh birth, marriage and death certificates at **www.col.statistics.gov.uk**

- For those of Scottish descent, images of 10 year Scottish census returns can be seen, from 1841 to 1901, at **www.scotlandspeople.gov.uk**

- Visit the website of the National Archives at **www.nationalarchives.gov.uk**

Computer Technology

Computers have proved a modern miracle for genealogists because of the considerable amount of data they can store. You could always take a computer course to enable you to learn the basics.

There are many genealogy programs available to buy, which will help you with your work. Make sure whatever you purchase is compatible either with your PC or your Apple Macintosh.

You could start with a simple shareware (free) one called PAF (Personal Ancestral File), which can be downloaded from the Church of Latter-Day Saints' site (www.familysearch.org).

TOP TIPS

GEDCOM

Genealogical Data Communications (GEDCOM) is a generic, database format designed to allow users to share family history database files between differing genealogy software programs.

GEDCOM files can be shared with others easily via e-mail attachment or on a disk. They can be converted for use in genealogy companion software programs and utilities that will create things like speciality charts, books, scrapbooks and websites.

- To create a GEDCOM file (in most programs), go to 'File, Export to GEDCOM' and create a new file with a '.ged' file extension after the name.

- To read another person's GEDCOM file (in most programs), go to 'File, Import from GEDCOM' and create a new database file that can be opened in your genealogy software program.

This will not merge with your existing database file unless you indicate that you wish for the two files to be merged.

You can buy different programs through the advertisements in genealogical magazines. If at all possible, go to a Family History Fair to see a demonstration of the different ones.

If you are British, don't be persuaded into buying an expensive program with lots of disks: most of the information will be American. Also, if you want your data to be transferable, you need to make sure it can be produced in the standard GEDCOM format.

"If you are British, don't be persuaded into buying an expensive program with lots of disks: most of the information will be American"

Collating material

Researching and recording your family history will require a certain amount of discipline on your part. There are thousands of excuses you can use for *not* sitting down and doing a bit of research or writing.

Set aside an amount of time regularly and you will soon get into a routine and start to see results. Don't be daunted by the amount of information that you think you need.

Even just doing an hour a day will soon bring about results, and you will love the buzz you get when you make your first major discovery or find a fresh new lead.

When recording results, don't just write down names and dates: this can make the work seem boring. Build up a picture of the lives of your ancestors as you go.

If you know their occupation, try to find out whether they were likely to have belonged to a trade association, whether or not they were married, what their life was like and more. Being a family historian is also like being a detective - you have to decide what evidence you want to use and what to leave out.

Come to a dead end?

If you can't find the information you are looking for, it could be that the spelling of a name is different. Make sure you check all spelling variations. For example, Randall could be Randell, Randle, Rawndell, Raundle, Rondal, Reondle, Andell, Rundill and much more - use your imagination!

There could be many other reasons too. For example, the mother's name on the birth certificate might not be the one she married under, or a man might have changed his name for a legacy inheritance (or to avoid the police, his wife or the army).

A will might not have been proved in the year a person died: it sometimes takes years to settle an estate. An apparently affluent person might not even have left a will.

"If you can't find the information you are looking for, it could be that the spelling of a name is different"

If you are really stuck in one place, try leaving it and moving onto a different piece of information. Ask others for advice if you are really desperate to find something out.

A member of a local society may be able to help you. Alternatively, the Family Records Centre occasionally holds a series of family history 'surgeries'. These are intended to help people who have hit a brick wall with their research. Call 020 8392 5300 for more details.

Red Herrings

Here some common things which may throw you off track:

- Biddy could be Bridget, or a term to describe an old woman
- Bessie could mean Elizabeth or an interfering old woman
- Elizabeth could also be Lizzie, Libby, Betty, Beth, Liza or Eliza
- Tillie or Mattie is Matilda
- Nancy is Ann
- Polly (or Molly) is Mary Anne (or Mary)
- Patty (or Matty) is Martha, not Patricia until 1920 plus
- Dolly or Dora is Dorothy
- Nellie is Ellen or Eleanor or Helen
- Bert is Albert or Herbert or Robert - Bertie may be Bertram
- Jenny or Jinny is Jane or Jean or Joan or Janet (Jessie in Scotland)
- Cissie might be Cicely or sister

Meeting with others

For expert help and advice from people interested in the subject, many professional organisations have been established. They cater for beginners to advanced genealogists.

One of the most important is the Society of Genealogists, who maintain a vast library of research material and publications from around the world. They also run lectures and provide research advice for beginners. Society of Genealogists, 14 Charterhouse Buildings, Goswell Road, London, EC1M 7BA, 020 7251 8799, www.sog.org.uk

Family history societies can provide a ready-made support network of other genealogists working in your area. The Federation of Family History Societies (www.ffhs.org.uk) can also provide useful contact details.

"Most family history societies hold regular meetings and are happy to welcome new members"

Most family history societies hold regular meetings and are happy to welcome new members to their activities and events. These range from talks by members on their own research, visiting speakers and professional genealogists and even excursions to record offices or other institutions.

Family history centres are maintained by the Church of the Latter-Day Saints, where printed or microfilm copies of genealogical sources are stored. Specific material can be requested and ordered in, if your research takes you away from the local area.

You might find that there are some adult education classes in family history being held near you at a local college, university, library or record office. Here you will learn a little more about the subject you are studying.

You will also meet like-minded people in your area, who may even be able to help with your research. The tutor is a good person to befriend as they can guide you if you appear to have reached a dead end.

"You might find that there are some adult classes in family history being held near you"

Finally, family history fairs are a popular way of finding out more about genealogy. They are designed to allow researchers to meet representatives from major institutions, societies and organisations.

Many of the larger fairs are accompanied by lecture programmes, and are great fun for beginners looking for inspiration and further guidance. Try searching on the Internet for one being held near you.

"**Family history fairs are designed to allow researchers to meet representatives from major institutions, societies and organisations**"

Understanding the Terms

The further back you search, the more likely it is that you will encounter some unfamiliar terms. For example, some family relationships and titles which show social status have different meanings now than they did in the 17th and 18th centuries.

Here are a few of the common terms:

- Mother - while it may be used in the modern sense, it might also refer to a mother-in-law or stepmother. Father, daughter and son are subject to the same variations

- Daughter-in-law - this term might have the same significance it has today or it might identify a stepchild. 'In-law' simply signified any relationship established by marriage

- Sister or brother - these may have the same implications as they do today. Equally, they may refer to a stepbrother or sister, a brother or sister-in-law, or to the husband of a sister, stepsister or sister-in-law. Another interpretation is a 'brother in the church' or a good friend

- Nephew - while this term was usually used with its modern meaning, it sometimes referred to a niece or even a male or female grandchild in early records

- Cousin - this was a general term used to refer to any relative outside the immediate family circle. Usually, it referred to a niece or nephew. Confusing this with today's meaning could seriously distort your research

- First cousin - used to be someone who has two of the same grandparents. A second cousin was someone who has the same great-grandparents, so a third cousin was someone whose great-great-grandparents are the same. Nowadays, however, the meaning is different, so be aware of this

- Spinster - up to the 18th century, this term referred to any woman who lived alone, whether she was single or a widow. Today, this word identifies a woman who has never married

- Junior, senior, II, etc. - these post-name labels were used to distinguish family members with the same name, often uncles and nephews. They did not imply a father-son relationship as they do now

  In small towns they might even have been used to distinguish persons of the same name but who weren't related at all

  The designations were not permanent. If Martin Cobb, Sr., died or moved away, Martin Cobb, Jr. became 'Sr.' and Martin Cobb III became 'Jr.'

- Gentleman - a descendant of an aristocratic family, who received his income from the rental of lands. He was a member of the landed gentry

Strictly speaking, if the son of a gentleman left home to become a tradesman, he lost his title. However, if he took up a profession such as law or the ministry, he was still considered a gentleman

- Esq. - an abbreviation for 'Esquire,' which referred to a member of the English gentry ranking just below a knight. Originally, it identified a candidate for knighthood who served as attendant to a knight. Today, it often refers to a member of the law profession

- Master - a title applied to a boy too young to be called Mr

Wise Words ❶
Don't get caught out by a change in meaning that has occurred between the date of the record and modern times. You could put an entirely erroneous slant on a relationship!

Drawing a Family Tree

Now that you have uncovered lots of fascinating information about your family history, you will want to record it in a family tree. You will already have decided which side you are recording: your mother's or father's.

Your family tree can be displayed horizontally, vertically or in a circular fashion. The most common version is vertical, with the earliest known ancestor at the top and successive generations arranged in horizontal levels below. It is then possible to see at a glance what family information you have discovered.

Begin with the birth of the eldest child on the left-hand side of the tree and so on along the line to the youngest at the right-hand side. Fill in dates of births, deaths and marriages.

A marriage is indicated by an equals sign (=). A short vertical line coming down from a married couple then meets a horizontal line at right angles, along which children are placed.

Most people start at the left with the eldest child, then work along to the right. Sometimes you will find all the males grouped together on the left, in order of birth, followed by all the females.

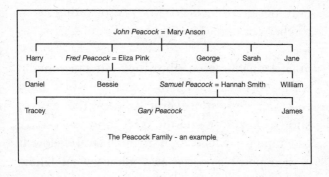

The Peacock Family - an example

Creating a Scrapbook

A family tree is not the only way to document your past; there are many other ideas for using the information you have researched. Why not create a regular family newsletter about your search, or even publish a book?

You might want to donate your account to genealogical libraries and societies, so that others may benefit from your work. Another lovely idea is to create a scrapbook containing photographs and other memorabilia. It doesn't have to be complicated to make; just follow our simple guide.

Creating a scrapbook has become such a popular pastime that in the world of crafts, it has become a craft of its own, known as 'scrapbooking'. It is a wonderful way to record special events and occasions. Like a colourful diary, it is a way to keep memories alive forever. You can work on it alone, or join with others to swap ideas.

The most important thing about the materials needed for scrapbooking is that they must be of sufficient quality to preserve your photographs and memorabilia. All albums, card, paper, paper, pens and glue must be acid-free. If not, the acid will deteriorate the paper and turn photographs yellow and faded.

Most craft companies and specialist scrapbooking companies will sell scrapbooking products. Look for the terms 'acid-free', 'photo-safe' or 'archival quality'. You will also need basic materials such as scissors, glue, and various coloured pens, as well as a variety of embellishments such as wire, ribbon, fabric, stickers and buttons.

Now you are ready to start. You can either work straight onto a pre-bound scrapbook or work on separate pieces of card, called 'layouts'.

On your page or sheet of coloured card, decide the theme of your page; for instance, will it be dedicated to a certain member of the family or a group? Choose the photographs you want to feature and decide whether you want to 'crop' them - cut edges off to remove unnecessary background or people.

Never crop polaroids, as they contain chemicals which will leak out, or heritage photographs, which are valuable and may be the only copy. You might want to mount the photos onto a slightly bigger piece of coloured paper or card, to provide a border. This is known as 'matting'.

When you want to place the photos, decide where you want them to go on the page. Is there a specific person or place that you want to feature? If so, fix them prominently on the page. Leaving room for a title, glue the photos down when happy with the position.

Now you can add a title, such as 'The Cobbold Family', or 'Summer Holiday '98'. You can draw this in fancy handwriting, use stick-on letters or even print it off in a swirly font and stick it on.

Now is your chance to be creative with your scrapbook. Why not add little bits of memorabilia, such as theatre tickets from a play the person being featured went to see. Or add little notes, quotations, poems or song lyrics onto the pages. This is known as 'journalling'.

You might want to include a drawing of your family tree somewhere in the scrapbook. You could also add beads, buttons and charms to the page, to liven it up. Be careful not to overdo it though.

Now you have a lasting memento of your family. Why not make another one and give it to a relative as a wonderful gift?

If you want to have a go at creating your own scrapbook, then a good place to start is looking for relevant books. 'Start Scrapbooking' by Joy Aitman (Search Press, £6.95) is a great place to begin.

Who to turn to

There are plenty of organisations that can help in your search for family history information.

England and Wales
- **Family Records Centre (FRC)**, 1 Myddelton Street, London EC1R 1UW, 020 8392 5300, www.familyrecords.gov.uk/frc

- **The National Archives (Public Records Office)**, Ruskin Avenue, Kew, Richmond, Surrey, TW9 4DU, 020 8876 3444, www.nationalarchives.gov.uk

- **The Borthwick Institute of Historical Research**, University of York, Heslington, York YO10 5DD, 01904 321166, www.york.ac.uk/inst/bihr

- **Guild of One-Name Studies (GOONS)**, Box G, 14 Charterhouse Buildings, Goswell Road, London EC1M 7BA

- **The British Library Newspaper Library**, Colindale Avenue, London NW9 5HE

- **Postal Application Office, Office for National Statistics**, General Register Office, Smedley Hydro, Southport, Merseyside PR8 2HH

- **Society of Genealogists**, 14 Charterhouse Buildings, Goswell Road, London, EC1M 7BA, 020 7251 8799, www.sog.org.uk

- **British Library Newspaper Library**, Colindale Avenue, London NW9 5HE, 020 7412 7353, www.bl.uk/collection/newspaper

- **Principal Probate Registry**, First Avenue House, 42-49 High Holborn, London WC1, 020 7947 6939, www.courtservice.gov.uk

- **Imperial War Museum**, Lambeth Road, London SE1 6HZ, 020 7416 5348, www.iwm.org.uk

- **Federation of Family History Societies**, PO Box 2425, Coventry CV5 6YX, 070 4149 2032, www.ffhs.org.uk/general/members/index.htm

- **The Institute of Heraldic and Genealogical Studies**, Northgate, Canterbury, Kent CT1 1BA

- **The Association of Genealogists and Researchers in Archives (AGRA)**, 29 Badgers Close, Horsham, West Sussex RH12 5RU.

Scotland
- **New Register House**, Edinburgh EH1 3YT

Ireland

- **General Register Office**, Joyce House, 8-11 Lombard Street East, Dublin 2

- **General Register Office for Northern Ireland**, 49-55 Chichester Street, Belfast BT1 4HL

- **The National Archives of Ireland** (Bishop Street, Dublin 8) or **The Public Record Office of Northern Ireland** (66 Balmoral Avenue, Belfast BT9 6NY, Northern Ireland)

And finally

So I hope you have been sufficiently inspired to go and start researching your own family history. Genealogy used to be a very isolated pursuit but now there are many people involved and it is possible to make lots of rewarding and varied friendships from this fascinating pastime.

Not only that, but you will have a lifelong interest which can yield unbelievable results; from discovering you are related to the Queen, to realising that you are descended from a rock star or a convict! No other hobby can promise such unusual results that could turn out to be more interesting than your wildest dreams!

After all, they say truth is stranger than fiction, so go and start exploring your family history...

Further

• •

Updates to this guide can be found at:
www.quick123.co.uk/familytree

Try these books and magazines for more
information on how to research your family tree.

Books
Dictionary of Genealogy (5th ed)
by Terrick V.H. Fitzhugh (A&C Black, 1998)

Tracing Your Family Tree
by Jean Cole and John Titford
(Countryside Books, £11.95)

Teach Yourself Tracing Your Family Tree
by Stella Colwell (Hodder & Stoughton, £8.99)

Writing Up Your Family History
by John Titford (Countryside Books, £6.99)

Start Scrapbooking
by Joy Aitman (Search Press, £6.99)

First Steps in Family History,
guided by Eve McLaughlin (Countryside Books, £7.95)

reading

. . . .

The Female Line by Margaret Ward
(Countryside Books, £7.95)

Magazines
Family Tree Magazine (ABM Publishing Ltd);
www.family-tree.co.uk

Practical Family History (ABM Publishing Ltd);
www.family-tree.co.uk/sister.htm

Family History Monthly
(Diamond Publishing Group Ltd); for subscription
information email: janice@dpgsubs.co.uk

Ancestors (The National Archives);
www.ancestorsmagazine.co.uk

The Genealogists' Magazine;
www.sog.org.uk/genmag

Family History News and Digest
(Federation of Family History Societies); www.ffhs.org.uk

Various journals published by
Family History Societies

Also available from

Quick123™

•GUIDES TO EVERYTHING•

- Get a Good Night's Sleep
- How to Protect Yourself from Identity Theft
- 25 Ways to Boost Your Income
- Get Started On eBay
- Get Out of Debt - and stay out
- Lose a Stone - and keep it off

and many more.....

For a list of titles and products go to
www.quick123.co.uk